Endorsements for the Church Questions Series

"Christians are pressed by very real questions. How does Scripture structure a church, order worship, organize ministry, and define biblical leadership? Those are just examples of the questions that are answered clearly, carefully, and winsomely in this new series from 9Marks. I am so thankful for this ministry and for its incredibly healthy and hopeful influence in so many faithful churches. I eagerly commend this series."

R. Albert Mohler Jr., President, The Southern Baptist Theological Seminary

"Sincere questions deserve thoughtful answers. If you're not sure where to start in answering these questions, let this series serve as a diving board into the pool. These minibooks are winsomely to-the-point and great to read together with one friend or one hundred friends."

Gloria Furman, author, *Missional Motherhood* and *The Pastor's Wife*

"As a pastor, I get asked lots of questions. I'm approached by unbelievers seeking to understand the gospel, new believers unsure about next steps, and maturing believers wanting help answering questions from their Christian family, friends, neighbors, or coworkers. It's in these moments that I wish I had a book to give them that was brief, answered their questions, and pointed them in the right direction for further study. Church Questions is a series that provides just that. Each booklet tackles one question in a biblical, brief, and practical manner. The series may be called Church Questions, but it could be called 'Church Answers.' I intend to pick these up by the dozens and give them away regularly. You should too."

Juan R. Sanchez, Senior Pastor, High Pointe Baptist Church, Austin, Texas

"Where can we Christians find reliable answers to our common questions about life together at church—without having to plow through long, expensive books? The Church Questions booklets meet our need with answers that are biblical, thoughtful, and practical. For pastors, this series will prove a trustworthy resource for guiding church members toward deeper wisdom and stronger unity."

Ray Ortlund, President, Renewal Ministries

What If I Don't Like My Church's Music?

Church Questions

Can Women Be Pastors?, Greg Gilbert

Does It Matter What I Believe?, Samuel James

Does the Gospel Promise Health and Prosperity?, Sean DeMars

Does the Old Testament Really Point to Jesus?, David M. King

How Can I Be Sure I'm Saved?, Jeremy Pierre

How Can I Begin to Teach the Bible?, David Helm

How Can I Encourage My Pastors?, Carmyn Zamora

How Can I Get More Out of My Bible Reading?, Jeremy Kimble

How Can I Grow in Hospitality?, Keri Folmar

How Can I Love Church Members with Different Politics?, Jonathan Leeman and Andy Naselli

How Can I Make the Most of Sunday Services?, Erin Wheeler

How Can I Serve My Church?, Matthew Emadi

How Can Women Thrive in the Local Church?, Keri Folmar

How Do I Disciple Others?, J. Garret Kell

How Do I Fight Sin and Temptation?, J. Garret Kell

How Do I Get Started in Evangelism?, Mack Stiles

Is God Really Sovereign?, Conrad Mbewe

Is Hell Real?, Dane Ortlund

Should I Be a Missionary?, Andy Johnson

What Do Deacons Do?, Juan Sanchez

What If I Don't Like My Church's Music?, Matthew Boswell

What If I'm Discouraged in My Evangelism?, Isaac Adams

What If I've Been Hurt by My Church?, Daniel P. Miller

What Is a Church?, Matthew Emadi

What Is the Church's Mission?, Jonathan Leeman

What Should I Do Now That I'm a Christian?, Sam Emadi

What Should I Look for in a Church?, Alex Duke

Who's in Charge of the Church?, Sam Emadi

Why Should I Be Baptized?, Bobby Jamieson

Why Should I Give to My Church?, Jamie Dunlop

Why Should I Join a Church?, Mark Dever

What If I Don't Like My Church's Music?

Matthew Boswell

CROSSWAY®

WHEATON, ILLINOIS

What If I Don't Like My Church's Music?

Published by Crossway
1300 Crescent Street
Wheaton, Illinois 60187

Cover image and design: Jordan Singer

First printing 2025

Printed in the United States of America

All emphases in Scripture quotations have been added by the author.

Trade paperback ISBN: 978-1-4335-9204-1
ePub ISBN: 978-1-4335-9206-5
PDF ISBN: 978-1-4335-9205-8

Library of Congress Cataloging-in-Publication Data

Names: Boswell, Matt, author.
Title: What if I don't like my church's music? / Matt Boswell.
Description: Wheaton, Illinois: Crossway, 2025. | Series: Church questions | Includes bibliographical references and index.
Identifiers: LCCN 2025005599 (print) | LCCN 2025005600 (ebook) | ISBN 9781433592041 (trade paperback) | ISBN 9781433592058 (pdf) | ISBN 9781433592065 (epub)
Subjects: LCSH: Music in churches. | Church music—Protestant churches. | Public worship.
Classification: LCC ML3001 .B747 2025 (print) | LCC ML3001 (ebook) | DDC 782.2/2—dc23/eng/20250423
LC record available at https://lccn.loc.gov/2025005599
LC ebook record available at https://lccn.loc.gov/2025005600

Crossway is a publishing ministry of Good News Publishers.

BP 34 33 32 31 30 29 28 27 26 25
15 14 13 12 11 10 9 8 7 6 5 4 3 2 1

Oh sing to the Lord a new song;
  sing to the Lord, all the earth!
Sing to the Lord, bless his name;
  tell of his salvation from day to day.
Declare his glory among the nations,
  his marvelous works among all the
    peoples!

Psalm 96:1–3

Some of my earliest and fondest memories involve singing in church. I can still see my dad singing on the front row before he got up to preach. He belted out each chorus, bouncing on his toes and lifting his eyebrows. I remember my mom arrayed in a blue robe, perched in the choir loft, and brimming with joy as she sang anthems to the Lord. I recall standing on my tiptoes as I sang beside older saints. They held our worn-out hymnals with their worn-out hands as they joined their voices with the rest of the congregation.

I cherish these memories. The well-worn melodies and theologically rich lyrics nurtured my understanding of Scripture and fueled my love for the Savior.

You may not have grown up in a church as I did, but if you've been a Christian for any amount of time, I'm sure you also have meaningful memories of singing with God's people.

Every Lord's Day, I show up at church full of anticipation. I'm eager to serve and be served by the gift of congregational song.

But this isn't the case for everyone. Church music is sometimes—both literally and figuratively—a clanging cymbal of frustration. I've known some Christians for whom singing was their least favorite part of corporate worship. They stood with arms crossed and lips sealed, basically holding their breath until the music was over.

What about you? Do you see congregational singing as a gift to enjoy or a burden to bear? Are you struggling to sing with God's people?

We can struggle with the music in our churches for many reasons. Perhaps the music in your church doesn't sound like that of the church down the street, with its seamless production and spotless execution. Maybe the church you have long called home keeps the lights at full strength during the service, so you feel too "seen" as you sing. It might be that the volume of the instruments is intentionally kept low and you feel too "heard." Or maybe the instrumental volume is much too high, so it's all you can hear!

Perhaps you miss the hymns of your childhood, the choruses of your college experience, or the songs of a previous church. You wonder why your church doesn't sing the songs you're familiar with. Maybe your church has weathered a contentious "worship war," and the conflict has soured your joy. Maybe the music has been changed, and now you find it too simplistic or too complex, too much of this or too little of that. Or perhaps you struggle with your church's music because of the clumsy string of wrong notes, out-of-tune guitars, and fumbled entrances.

No matter what frustrations you may have with your church's music, I hope to help you navigate those challenges and point you to some of the glorious reasons you have to lift your voice in song during worship. My hope is that by the time you finish reading this book, you won't be able to wait until the next time you get to sing with your church.

The glorious truth is that all who are in Christ have joined the choir of the redeemed and have been given a song of salvation. Because of Christ, we have ten thousand reasons to sing.

I've invested the majority of my life participating in, leading, thinking about, and even writing church music. The goal of this book is to help you understand the Bible's vision for what it looks like for God's people to sing together. I want to convince you of the goodness of congregational singing and the vital role that you play in it. Along the way I also hope to give some practical counsel on how to address your heart if your church's music isn't your preference, grates on your nerves, or frustrates you.

Dozens of Scripture passages address the topic of music and singing. We'll consider many of them in the pages ahead. But as we do, I'd like to make Psalm 96:1–3 our "home base." David's words summarize the essential truths that help us understand church music rightly—truths that can help our souls if we don't like our church's music.

> Oh sing to the LORD a new song;
> sing to the LORD, all the earth!
> Sing to the LORD, bless his name;
> tell of his salvation from day to day.
> Declare his glory among the nations,
> his marvelous works among all the
> peoples! (Ps. 96:1–3)

In this psalm, David gives us three reasons why Christians sing together: singing is *an act of worshiping God*, *an act of discipling others*, and ultimately *an act of witnessing to the world*.

An Act of Worshiping God

Singing is an act of worship. David makes this clear in Psalm 96:1: "Oh sing *to the LORD* a new song." For the Christian, singing is never *just* singing. It's so much more. Whether we sing alone, at home with our families, or with our churches, our singing is first and foremost an offering unto God.

Because singing is worship, it isn't ultimately for us; it's for God. We sing for a divine audience. In fact, did you notice that in Psalm 96 David calls us to sing to the Lord three times? The Lord of all creation condescends to hear our song (Ps. 40:1). It really is quite stunning. We must worship him not only with narrative and prose, but also with music and poetry, melody and harmony, rhythm and rhyme.

Psalm 96 introduces us to two important truths we need to remember if we're struggling with the music in our churches. First, God commands singing. Second, he commands singing because church music is ultimately about worshiping him, not meeting our preferences.

Commanded by God

Why do Christians sing?

I realize this might seem like a silly question, but have you ever stopped and thought about it? Of course, there are untold numbers of reasons why Christians sing. We sing as a practice of prayer, to express emotion, to communicate God's truth creatively, to celebrate the gospel, and the list goes on. But the ultimate reason Christians sing is because God commands us to do it.

We don't approach God on our terms or according to our preferences. He invites us to worship him on his terms. He dictates not only that we must worship him but how we worship him. One of the ways God has ordained that we should worship him is by song. That's why the Christian faith is a singing faith. We sing as an act of obedience. We sing because our singing pleases God.

In fact, when we consider the sum of the commands to sing in Scripture and the role singing plays at so many critical points in redemptive history, we have to conclude that our God really, really likes to hear his people sing. Singing saints bring deep joy to the heart of God—whether they're singing psalms of praise, hymns of devotion, lyrics of lament, or melodies from hearts made new. Just as my heart swells when I hear my children singing in our home, the heart of the Father is stirred by his sons and daughters singing to him in love and devotion.

If you're struggling to resonate with your church's music, remember that our circumstances don't change what God expects of his people. Singing isn't a divine suggestion; it is a holy commandment. And like all of God's commands, it's not a burden to weigh us down but a law that lifts us up. Christian singing is a harmony of duty and delight. Just as God delights in our singing, our singing fuels our delight in God.

Commanded for God

I had become a Christian some years before, but when I was fifteen, the Lord gripped my heart with his grace in such a profound way that the only thing I knew to do was to sing. I started writing songs about who God is, what God had done, and what he was doing in my life. I had something to sing about. God's love causes the silent heart to sing.

When we enjoy God, our hearts are compelled to praise him, and that act of praise completes our joy. Have you ever eaten at a restaurant or watched a movie that you *had* to tell someone about? Why do we get that feeling? C. S. Lewis explains it well: "I think we delight to praise what we enjoy because *the praise not merely expresses but completes the enjoyment; it is its appointed consummation*."[1] If your heart has been remade, reformed, and recalibrated by the love of God in Christ, then the deepest part of you can't help but sing about what God has done.

This is another reason why God commands us to sing. For God's people, singing is more than just melody making and lyric reciting. Singing is an "appointed consummation" of our delight in God. David also makes this point plainly in Psalm 96:2: We must "bless [God's] name." Singing isn't ultimately about us. It's ultimately about extolling God for his glory.

Too often we get this upside down. We treat the music in our churches as if it's there to cater to our preferences, meet our needs, or give us a certain feeling. But that's putting ourselves at the center of our songs. If you don't like your church's music, that's okay. It's not really *for* you. It's a vehicle for you to bless God's name with other redeemed sinners.

In fact, David presses this point even further by reminding us that we should sing to God "a new song" (Ps. 96:1). He's not suggesting that every Sunday you need a fresh batch of hymns you've never sung before. A new song is a "fresh song responding to a freshly received, fresh experience."[2] In other words, singing to God a new song means our musical worship isn't fueled by having our preferences satisfied but by responding to God's daily grace. In the same way that God's mercies are new every morning, each day brings new reasons for praise. Every published hymnal has a beginning and an end, but the hymnal for Christ's church has no back cover. His mercy is endless; so also are the songs that celebrate his mercy. The Lord continually gives his people reason to sing.

This point can be particularly helpful if you're struggling with the *style* of your church's music. Style isn't irrelevant. In fact, there may be some real stylistic issues in your church's music that make it difficult for you to participate in the singing. The tunes could be difficult to sing. The rhythm could be challenging. The range of notes might reach far too high and then sink way too low. The songs might be set in keys that make them frustrating for nonmusical people to join in. The music could be too loud and showy. Or maybe you think the leadership is so quiet you don't feel like you're being led at all.

Those are real issues. But they're not ultimate ones. We don't sing because we like the music, because it's led particularly well, or because it fits our style. We sing because it's appropriate to respond to fresh grace with fresh songs.

The fact that singing is ultimately about worshiping God and not satisfying ourselves also shapes how we should think about our churches' song selection. This may also be a point of frustration for you. Perhaps you're bothered that your church sings only old songs when so many wonderful new songs exist—or vice versa.

As I explained above, when David commands that we sing a "new song" to the Lord, he doesn't mean we should sing only songs that were written in the last decade. His point is that all our singing should be a fresh response to God's grace. Sometimes that means singing something genuinely new. At the time David wrote Psalm 96, he couldn't have imagined the number of songs praising the one true God that would be composed in the millennia ahead. New songs would emerge from far beyond the borders of Israel as God's new covenant people began to praise him in a diversity of styles and genres and across cultural and linguistic boundaries. Christian music began to feature the talking drum of West Africa, the high-church hymn of London, the buzzing sitar of northern India, the Gaelic psalm singing of the Hebrides, and the blues guitar of Muscle Shoals, Alabama. Just as God's new mercies visit us daily, new songs should be a welcomed addition to our ever-expanding hymnals.

But that doesn't mean old hymns should be boxed up and stored in the church attic. Such songs are a meaningful part of Christian worship. We should sing them with as much zeal as we sing new songs—they may be well-worn, but that's because they've ministered truth to so many saints. Church history contains a repository of musical riches that we should continue to sing. Historic hymns remind us that we are not the first generation to have wrestled, prayed, lamented, and praised through life. Many of us remember particular songs from our past that carried us through specific seasons.

I'm sure no one church gets the balance of old and new just right. You might be struggling because you wish your church had more of one and less of the other. But whether we're singing something old or something new, what matters is praising God for the work he's done and continues to do.

Here's the bottom line: What should you do if you don't like your church's music? Sing anyway! Remember, you're not singing for you, you're singing for God. If you meditate on his character and work you'll realize that you have ten thousand reasons to lift your voice. As you consider the privilege of singing—the who, the what, and the why of it all—you'll understand that congregational singing is more than an arrangement of melodies and lyrics performed by a group of strangers for your personal benefit. Congregational singing is an act of worship offered to the living God by a group of fellow believers who participate together in Christ by faith.

The next time a service begins, try not to see the songs as a prelude to preaching. Don't think of them as a warm-up exercise before an exposition. Don't focus on the elements of the music that frustrate you or don't align with your preferences. Instead, focus first and foremost on what you're doing in that moment. You're offering praise to the one true God. So treat singing seriously, like something you have been commanded to do before the Lord. Join your voice with fellow saints and sing as an expression of worship with your heart full.

> O worship the King, all glorious above;
> O gratefully sing his power and his love;
> Our shield and defender, the Ancient of
> Days,
> Pavilioned in splendor and girded with
> praise.[3]

An Act of Discipling Others

David's invitation to praise God in Psalm 96 isn't an auditioning call for solo performers. He's summoning a choir composed of every tribe, tongue, and nation. "Sing to the LORD, all the earth!" (Ps. 96:1).

The Israelites would have understood David's invitation as anticipating a day when Gentiles would join their voices to songs of praise to Yahweh, who is "great . . . and greatly to be praised," the one true God who is to be "feared above all gods" (Ps. 96:4). Individual praise has its place, of course. But in Psalm 96, David envisions the songs of a new creation coming from a global choir.

With the resurrection of Christ, the day David longed for has come. The gospel draws men and women from every tribe, tongue, and nation into local churches to lift up their voices in song. When we gather to sing, we're not soloists but choir members who have responded to God's own invitation to join with all the earth in praise.

Some people view the musical portion of corporate worship as a personal time set aside for just them and God. I've heard more than one music director encourage all those in the congregation to close their eyes and imagine it's just them and Jesus in the room. But that idea runs roughshod over the Bible's vision for *corporate* worship. Christian singing isn't a private act for personal enjoyment. It's an act of service. If you're struggling to "like" your church's music, you may need to remember that your singing isn't designed to be a souped-up quiet time but an act of service to fellow Christians. It isn't just for God; it's also *for* others.

A Ministry of Telling

Engaging in the work of congregational singing is one way every believer builds up the body of Christ. Not everyone preaches. We don't all pray or publicly read Scripture. But each of us who is in Christ can have an effective ministry edifying the whole church through song.

In Psalm 96:2, David invites the earth to "tell" of God's salvation. This means that congregational singing is a "ministry of telling." As we sing, we proclaim the truths of our faith to one another. God may be our primary audience, but he's not our only audience. The direction of our singing is vertical *and* horizontal; it's both Godward and manward.[4] As we extol God for his mercy, we are at the same time telling one another of the wondrous things that God has done.

God's people have always functioned this way. Exodus records how God rescued his people from slavery so they might be free to worship him. The first thing Moses and the people did on the other side of deliverance was to stop and sing. They reminded one another through song what God had done to redeem them.

The same principle holds true in the New Testament. In Colossians 3, Paul instructs the believers in the church at Colossae how to live in love and harmony with one another. They fulfill that command by singing the truths of the gospel, the "word of Christ," to every other member: "Let the word of Christ dwell in you richly, teaching and admonishing one another in all wisdom, singing psalms and hymns and spiritual songs, with thankfulness in your hearts to God" (Col. 3:16).

We find the same teaching in Ephesians 5:18–21:

> And do not get drunk with wine, for that is debauchery, but be filled with the Spirit, addressing one another in psalms and hymns and spiritual songs, singing and making melody to the Lord with your heart, giving thanks always and for everything to God the Father in the name of our Lord Jesus Christ, submitting to one another out of reverence for Christ.

The God-directed ministry of praise and the others-directed ministry of edification are intimately linked throughout the New Testament.[5] This means that the goal of congregational singing is to glorify God *by* encouraging one another in song. It encompasses both aims.

Paul's teaching challenges our consumerism and confronts our ill-informed notion that the church's music is supposed to cater to our preferences or create in us a certain emotional response. God's design is for us to participate in producing the church's music, not just enjoy it. We gather to be part of a congregational choir, not attend a concert. When we understand this, our participation is less about whether we like the music and more about whether we will serve our brothers and sisters. In fact, when you read Colossians 3 and Ephesians 5, you begin to see that singing looks and sounds a lot like the work of discipling: helping others follow Jesus.

Since congregational singing is a "one another" ministry in the church, we should tailor our expectations for Sunday morning toward that end. We show up to hear and be heard by our brothers and sisters in the pews. Since we're singing to one another, the main thing we should want to hear on Sunday morning is the voice of the congregation. Perhaps you long for that and wish your church was more committed to that vision. But even if the musical leadership in your church isn't trying to elevate the congregation as the main thing that's heard on Sunday morning, don't let that stop you from singing loudly to encourage those around you while also listening eagerly to hear them sing as well.

The spiritual good we do in and for one another as we sing together is incalculable. I can affirm that from personal experience. As a pastor, I have the privilege of regularly preaching God's word. My job is a "ministry of telling." But each Sunday I am not only a participant in this ministry of telling but also a recipient of it. When people ask me in the days leading up to Sunday if I am ready to preach, I always reply, "I'm not ready until we sing," and I mean it. There is something about singing with our church family that stirs my soul. The saints around me are teaching me and encouraging me with God's word in those moments.

One of my favorite things to do in our worship service is to sing with full voice, bouncing on my toes with lifted eyebrows (just like my dad still does). I look around at the faces of my brothers and sisters who sing beside me and I'm reminded how many of these people that I know and love are singing through suffering and sorrows. This past Sunday, I sang with multiple loved ones who are battling terminal cancer, one friend offering his praise with borrowed breath while hooked up to an oxygen machine, a young father facing an unknown career future, a couple heartbroken over the decisions of a child, an elderly widow who desperately misses her husband, and the list goes on. I join my voice with theirs with an aim to minister to them—to sing with them as we stand on the truths we declare together.

My heart soars in those moments—nourished by the truths sung to me by fellow saints. As I walk up the stairs to preach the good news of Jesus, my soul is often carried there by the singing of others in the room.

Telling from Day to Day

As we consider our responsibility to serve others by singing the truth to them, we should take note of one last phrase in Psalm 96:2. We must "Sing to the LORD, . . . tell of his salvation *from day to day.*" In other words, we need to engage in this "ministry of telling" not only when we feel like it, when it's convenient, or when we're moved by the music. We need to do it day by day. We should tell others about God's salvation through song every time the church gathers. Your fellow church members need to hear you sing the gospel to them day by day and week by week.

We need to be reminded of the salvation God has given us in Christ every day. This gospel is the news that edifies us, the truth that builds us up, and our hope for the future. Charles Spurgeon, a well-known pastor in London in the nineteenth century, once said, "The gospel is the clearest revelation of [God], salvation outshines creation and providence; therefore let our praises overflow in that direction. Let us proclaim the glad tidings, and do so continually, never ceasing the blissful testimony."[6] What a precious gift to have the gospel on our lips. What a holy privilege to sing the good news of great joy to fellow members from Lord's Day to Lord's Day, helping them grow even more as worshiping disciples of Jesus.

If we approach church music as consumers, then we'll be continually asking questions such as "What do I like?" or "What do I get from this?" But when we walk into corporate worship, we should check our scorecards and shopping lists at the door. Congregational singing isn't about consumption. It's a time for us to contribute to the faith of other believers in the room by singing the gospel to them Sunday by Sunday.

Telling the Truth

As a pastor and someone deeply invested in church music, I've developed my own set of convictions for what makes for a good "church song." Each week, my goal for our church is that every song be (1) biblically faithful, (2) theologically rich, (3) beautifully devotional, (4) congregationally edifying, and (5) missionally intentional. Your church may have its own set of values. I'm simply putting my cards on the table, showing you the filter I and the other elders at my church use when we're assessing a song for congregational use.

I often visit churches that sing songs that don't align with my convictions. Sometimes I don't prefer the arrangements or the style of the songs, or I think the lyrics aren't as rich as they should be.

But I still sing. And I do it enthusiastically.

How? I look for lyrics that faithfully tell of the things God has done. I allow my soul to be nourished by the truths of Scripture reflected in the song. I search for what is beautiful in the tune and text. I scan the room to see how the song is ministering to others. I rejoice in the ways my brothers and sisters in Christ are being edified by the truth. I consider how non-Christians in the room might hear the truth of the gospel in a way that makes sense. I never cease to be discerning, but I join in worshiping. A particular song might not be in my preferred style or arrangement, but I worship according to the truth of the song, endeavoring to encourage my brothers and sisters around me with that truth. I want the words of worship theologian Harold Best to be true of me: "A mark of a mature Christian is that they are easily edified."[7]

Let me tell you a story about how good it can be for your soul to sing songs you don't prefer but that preach the same gospel you believe. Once a friend of mine was scheduled to give a testimony during a special service. The only trouble was that she sometimes stutters uncontrollably. So she decided to sing her testimony using a song that ministered to her personally. It's not a song I would have chosen for our church because it didn't meet some of the criteria I listed earlier. But that night, she sang as her husband played guitar. During the third verse she got choked up and couldn't sing, so the congregation stood and sang for her. Rivers of salt streamed down my face as I lifted my voice.

That was one of the most beautiful moments I remember singing with our church. Think of all I would have missed out on if I had just crossed my arms and gritted my teeth. May we be easily edified as the word of Christ dwells in us through song.

It may be that you're struggling with your church's music precisely because the theology of the lyrics is so flimsy or shallow that the focus of the songs has drifted from the main tenets of the Christian faith: the glory of God, the cross of Christ, the forgiveness of sins, the newness of life, and the hope of the resurrection. Maybe you're singing lyrics that make you scratch your head and you're worried the songs may even contradict the teachings of Scripture. If that sounds like the music at your church, I encourage you to talk with your pastor about your concerns and humbly ask what principles the church leaders consider when choosing the congregational songs. You want to approach such a conversation graciously and humbly, but recognize that singing is a big part of the church's teaching ministry. If the lyrics aren't teaching the truth or celebrating God's work in the gospel, those may be reasons enough to find a church that values truth in song and shares your biblical and theological convictions.

But if your church's songs are proclaiming the glorious truth that Christ died for sinners, then you have a reason to sing, even if you don't like your church's music.

Perhaps the next time you're singing a hymn, you'll notice someone around you with his or her mouth shut. Maybe that person has just received shattering news, recently lost a loved one, or is going through a spiritual desert. As you sing the glorious truths of the hymn to that believer, the Lord may work through your singing to renew his or her hope in Christ.

Most of my time is spent as a pastor, but I also serve as a professor of church music and worship. So if you will allow it, let me assign you a brief homework assignment. Do your own study of Colossians 3:16 and Ephesians 5:18–20. Continue to grow both in your understanding and your practice of singing as an expression of discipleship.

> Come, Christians, join to sing,
> Alleluia, Amen!
> Loud praise to Christ our King,
> Alleluia, Amen!
> Let all, with heart and voice,
> Before his throne rejoice;
> Praise is his gracious choice,
> Alleluia, Amen![8]

An Act of Witnessing to the World

A third reason we have to sing is as *a witness to the world.*

Psalm 96:3 tells us, "Declare his glory among the nations, his marvelous works among all the peoples!" In this verse, David gives us a clarion call to "say among the nations, 'The LORD reigns!'" (Ps. 96:10). One pastor explained David's exhortation this way: "The psalm teaches that worship should never be merely a private thing, something between ourselves and God only, but should also be that which leads to a missionary witness."[9]

There are at least two ways that singing is a declaration to the world: through the content of our songs and through the unity of our singing.

The Witness of Our Message

When I was in seminary, I had the privilege of taking a doctoral seminar with Tom Nettles, a legendary church historian. Nettles has a beautiful voice and is well known for breaking out into song in the middle of his lectures. One afternoon, I and another student took Nettles to lunch at a favorite haunt, where we learned that Nettles would sometimes sing even between bites of elk burger!

I had been a Christian for some time. I was even a pastor. But sitting in a public place with a professor who would spontaneously burst into song was a little beyond my comfort zone. What would people think about this distinguished elderly man and his two students singing at a lunch table in the middle of a restaurant?

He didn't care. He sang.

As he continued singing, I felt a change in my heart. I realized that he was singing because he had a song to sing. He couldn't stop the song from coming out. He declared the glory of the Lord among the nations—or at least among the people in the restaurant. That day, I learned an important lesson: the praises of the Lord are not something we should contain within the four walls of a church. We should proclaim them everywhere to everyone.

When the church gathers, we should expect that our songs will be overheard by those who have yet to trust in Christ as Savior (see 1 Cor. 14:24–25). Songs are like messengers carrying the good news of Jesus on the winds of melody and the wings of lyrics. Just as David wanted his songs to declare the goodness and faithfulness of God in his day, we, too, want to tell of his goodness and faithfulness that we have seen in the gospel.

Sometimes, before a service begins, I address those who are not Christians by saying, "If you are not yet a believer in Jesus, we don't expect you to sing these songs with us, but we do invite you to listen closely as we sing these truths like we believe them!" On one hand, this reminds the congregation that singing is the responsibility of every believer. On the other hand, it reminds us that unbelievers are present and they need to hear the good news of the gospel—and our corporate singing is a powerful apologetic for that gospel.

We want to tell our neighbors and our church visitors the marvelous works of God. We want to tell them about the steadfast love of God and his mercy in sending his one and only Son to seek and to save the lost. We declare the marvelous works of Christ in the incarnation, in his living and dying, and in his resurrection and ascension. We proclaim our hope in his coming return. And we do all of this as we sing to God and to one another.

Your church's music might not fit your style or satisfy all of your preferences. But does it faithfully declare the good news of the gospel? If so, then recognize that that music is achieving what God desires, and it may even have a hand in bringing an unbeliever to "[fall] on his face . . . [and] worship God" (1 Cor. 14:25). If that's true, it should be a joy for us to be able to participate in the church's music, even if we don't like it.

The Witness of Our Unity

The church's singing is powerful because we get to hear voices from different backgrounds, ethnicities, economic classes, and life stories. I'm sure that no two members of my church would pick the exact same music to sing on any given Sunday. But there we are, every member putting aside his or her preferences to come together and sing. John 13:35 says that the world will know we are Christians by our love for one another. Putting aside our deeply held preferences and musical tastes in order to sing together is one expression of that love.

We also manifest that love by forbearing with one another's weaknesses. Perhaps the musical leadership in your church simply isn't as gifted as that of the church down the road. Wrong notes, inconsistent rhythms, and clunky entrances may be the rule rather than the exception. That's okay. In Christ, we not only forgive one another's sins, we overlook one another's weaknesses—including musical weaknesses.

When we sing together week after week, this unified stream of praise to our Savior is one powerful way we declare the glory of God to those who are not in Christ. We offer outsiders not just our individual witness but a corporate witness. We demonstrate that God remakes our hearts individually but also as a people. We give them a glimpse of a new people united around the good news of God's work in Christ and the joy of knowing him.

It is in this spirit that we can echo the prayer of George Herbert:

> Let all the world in ev'ry corner sing,
> My God and King!

The heav'ns are not too high,
His praise may thither fly;
The earth is not too low,
His praises there may grow.
Let all the world in ev'ry corner sing,
My God and King![10]

A Prayer for You

Before you finish this book, I want you to know something: I have prayed for you.

I imagine that anyone who picks up a booklet entitled *What If I Don't Like My Church's Music?* is a lot like myself: Someone who cares deeply about church music and the gift of congregational singing. My home study is spilling over with books on corporate worship and the role music plays in it. I have devoted my life to learning about this practice. And yet I'm more aware than ever that I still have much to learn.

Given the brevity of this book, I'm sure you still have unanswered questions. I encourage you to follow up with a pastor in your church. Tell him how much you care about church music and that you'd like to understand even more how congregational singing is an act of worship, a means of discipleship, and a witness to the world. I'm sure he would love to talk with you further about how these principles find expression in your local church.

Ultimately, I prayed for you that when you put this book down you won't be able to wait until the next time you get to sing with your church.

On the next Lord's Day, I hope you'll sing from the bottom of your heart with gratitude to the Lord as an act of worship. I pray you'll sing to your brothers and sisters in Christ as you lend your voice to the work of building up other disciples. And finally, I pray that as you sing, the Lord will bring into your gathering many people to whom you can boldly declare the salvation of our God.

Notes

1. C. S. Lewis, *Reflections on the Psalms* (HarperCollins, 2017), 111 (emphasis added).
2. Alec Motyer, *Psalms by the Day: A New Devotional Translation* (Christian Focus, 2018), 271.
3. Robert Grant, "O Worship the King," 1833.
4. Derek Kidner, *Psalms 73–150*, Tyndale Old Testament Commentaries (IVP Academic, 2008), 379.
5. David Peterson, *Engaging with God: A Biblical Theology of Worship* (Eerdmans, 1992), 221.
6. C. H. Spurgeon, *The Treasury of David*, vol. 4 (Passmore & Alabaster, 1888), 181.
7. Chip Stam, Mike Cosper, and Harold Best, Worship Discussion 1, February 14, 2009, https://vimeo.com/3213820.
8. Christian H. Bateman, "Come, Christians, Join to Sing," 1843.
9. James Montgomery Boice, *Psalms*, vol. 2, Psalms 42–106 (Baker, 1994), 784.
10. George Herbert, "Let All the World in Every Corner Sing," 1633.

Scripture Index

IX 9Marks

Building Healthy Churches

9Marks exists to equip church leaders with a biblical vision and practical resources for displaying God's glory to the nations through healthy churches.

To that end, we want to see churches characterized by these nine marks of health:

1. Expositional Preaching
2. Gospel Doctrine
3. A Biblical Understanding of Conversion and Evangelism
4. Biblical Church Membership
5. Biblical Church Discipline
6. A Biblical Concern for Discipleship and Growth
7. Biblical Church Leadership
8. A Biblical Understanding of the Practice of Prayer
9. A Biblical Understanding and Practice of Missions

John Onwuchekwa
Sam Emadi
Mark Dever
How Can I Grow in Hospitality?
Keri Folmar
How Do I Get Started in Evangelism?
Mack Stiles
Who's in Charge of the Church?
Sam Emadi
How Can I Serve My Church?
Matthew Emadi